Substituting Ingredients

"A book which no experienced, as well as beginning, cook should be without. . . . The authors also provide remedies for kitchen disasters most cookbooks blithely assume will never happen."

—*Santa Barbara (CA) News-Press*

"At one time or another, we all have decided to make something, looked into our cupboard and discovered a missing ingredient. Now, there's help at hand. . . . *Substituting Ingredients* is the most comprehensive substitution list that I have seen."

—*New Haven (CT) Register*

"If you've ever started to bake and discovered when you're elbow-deep in flour that you're out of an ingredient, have I got a book for you. . . . I'm putting this book in a kitchen drawer where it will be handy when I need it."

—*Las Vegas Sun*

Substituting Ingredients

An A to Z Kitchen Reference

SECOND EDITION

by
Becky Sue Epstein
and
Hilary Dole Klein

The
Globe
Pequot
Press

Chester, Connecticut

Library of Congress Cataloging-in-Publication Data

Epstein, Becky Sue, 1952-
    Substituting ingredients: an A to Z kitchen reference / by Becky Sue Epstein and Hilary Dole Klein. — 2nd ed.
    p. cm.
  Includes index.
  ISBN 0-87106-164-3
  1. Cookery.   2. Ingredient substitutions (Cookery) I. Klein, Hilary Dole, 1945- . II. Title.
  TX652.E59 1992
  641.5—dc20   91-24150
                                                     CIP

Book design by Nancy Freeborn
Illustrations by Kathy Michalove/Pen & Ink
Manufactured in the United States of America
Second Edition/First Printing

Contents

Introduction 1

Tips for Successful Substituting 3

Substituting Ingredients A to Z 5

Too Much 105

Measurement Equivalents 107

Household Formulas 115

Introduction

Don't have an ingredient? *Substitute!*

Don't like something? *Substitute!*

Can't afford it? *Substitute!*

It's Sunday morning. You wake up and find yourself strangely filled with energy. You decide to make pancakes as a special treat for the family—the fluffy yet substantial kind of pancakes your mother made on Sundays. You can almost taste them. You reach for the cookbook where the recipe is marked by a turned-down, much bespattered page.

"Sour Milk Griddle Cakes," the recipe reads. You stop. Who, in his or her right mind, keeps sour milk around? You can almost feel the softness of the pancake in your mouth, smothered with real Vermont maple syrup. This is the only pancake recipe you want to use. What should you do?

It's a Friday evening. You've prepared a wonderful meal, straight out of Julia Child (well, almost), fit for a king. Fit, you hope, for an enchanting business dinner that will eventually bring you all the projects, raises, and promotions you've dreamed of. It's 7:30, and the guests are due any moment. The sauce needs only one final touch to complete its superb flavor. You reach for the cognac to dash in the required two tablespoons. Then you stop. You recall cousin Don finished off the cognac last weekend. What now?

Whether on a deserted island, in a rented vacation cottage, or at home with no time for a trip to the store, everyone has, at some time, been in this predicament: The recipe you're making calls for an ingredient you don't happen to have on hand.

1

After becoming frantic with problems like this once too often, we decided to do something about it and came up with something that we, as well as our friends, could benefit by: a book of substitutions. A year of research, questioning, and testing later, the first edition appeared. For this second edition we have added ingredients required for newly popular American regional and international cuisines, including Cajun, Mexican, Central American, Southeast Asian, French Provincial, Italian country, and Pacific Rim. We have also incorporated ingredient equivalents directly into the text.

Take into account your personal preferences and our modern cuisine with its increasing health consciousness. Use your own judgment when you choose between substitutes for a given ingredient. Generally, these are substitutions, not exact equivalents.

Simple? Yes!

With this guide in your kitchen, you need not despair. We have it covered, from allspice to zucchini. Just look up the next best thing and continue on with your cooking and baking.

Remember: It's better to substitute than omit!

Tips for Successful Substituting

Here are a few general things to note for successful results when substituting:

❖ Where several substitutes are given, we've tried to list them beginning with the best-tasting (and best-functioning) equivalent; but use your own preferences as a guide.

It's important to remember that substitutions which work in the oven may not work on top of the stove. And vice versa.

Baking

Certain substitutions are standard in baking recipes, one of the most obvious being that margarine can be used in place of shortening or butter without noticeably affecting the texture of the baked goods.

Baking times may vary, depending on the substitution, so be sure to monitor items and test for doneness.

When making substitutions in baking, try to keep the ratio of liquid ingredients to dry ingredients as close as possible to the original recipe.

Dairy Products

Except when needed for whipping, heavy cream and light cream can be used interchangeably. Yogurt or sour cream can be used for a tangier taste or a different fat content, although it's generally not a good idea to boil yogurt or sour cream: They can separate.

Fruits

When you're making a pie, one berry can be as flavorful as the next. And limes are as good as lemons in any recipe we can think of. Both are indispensable—a splash of either juice, for instance, will keep cut fruits and vegetables from turning brown.

We have substituted fruits by taste, which seemed the most appropriate method, especially when preparing non-baked items like drinks, salads, and sorbets. For cooking and baking, you will find that a fruit's size and textural differences affect cooking times and may alter the amount of fruit to be used in the recipe. For apples, especially, the type is important, both for taste and texture.

Herbs, Spices, and Flavorings

In general, 1 tablespoon of fresh herbs equals 1 teaspoon of dried herbs. When using dried herbs, crush them in the palm of your hand to release their flavors. If using dried substitutions, cook the dish 15 minutes after adding, then taste.

Wines and spirits are often used to add flavor. The alcohol evaporates quickly during cooking. For both red and white wines, stick to the drier, rather than sweet, varieties. Madeira, sherry, and port are used to add sweetness to specific cooking and baking recipes.

Make Your Own

You will notice recipes for common condiments, sauces, spice mixtures, and more throughout the book. Be adventurous and try them!

Substituting Ingredients
A to Z

A

Acorn Squash

= butternut squash

= pumpkin

Agar-Agar

= gelatin

Alfalfa Sprouts

= watercress

See Sprouts

Allspice

= ¼ teaspoon cinnamon and ½ teaspoon ground cloves

= ¼ teaspoon nutmeg, in baking

= black pepper, in cooking

❖ Almonds ❖

1 lb. shelled = 1 to 1½ cups

1 lb. in shells = 3½ cups

Angel Hair Pasta

See Pasta

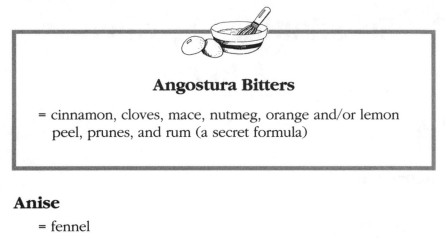

Angostura Bitters

= cinnamon, cloves, mace, nutmeg, orange and/or lemon peel, prunes, and rum (a secret formula)

Anise

= fennel

= dill

= cumin

Anise Seed or Star Anise

= fennel seed

= caraway seed (use more)

= chervil (use a lot more)

Apples, chopped, 1 cup

= 1 cup firm pears, chopped, plus 1 tablespoon lemon juice

❖ Apples ❖

1 lb. = 2 large apples

1 lb. = 2½ to 3 cups, sliced

Apples, sweet/mild
= golden delicious
= New Zealand Fuji
= red delicious
= Rome
= russet

Apples, tart
= Granny Smith
= Gravenstein

Apples, tart/sweet
= Jonathan
= McIntosh
= New Zealand Braeburn
= pippin
= Winesap

Arrowroot
= flour, up to a few tablespoons, for thickening
See Flour

Artichoke Hearts
= chayote, cooked and seasoned
= Jerusalem artichoke, also known as sunchoke
= kohlrabi, cooked

Arugula or Rocket
= Belgian endive
= endive
= escarole
= dandelion greens

Asian Pears

= pears

Azafran or Safflower

= saffron (use only a tiny bit)

B

Bacon

= smoked ham, in cooking

Baking Powder, 1 teaspoon double-acting

= $\frac{1}{2}$ teaspoon cream of tartar plus $\frac{1}{4}$ teaspoon baking soda

= $\frac{1}{4}$ teaspoon baking soda plus $\frac{1}{2}$ cup sour milk or cream or buttermilk; reduce some other liquid from recipe

= $\frac{1}{4}$ teaspoon baking soda plus 2 more eggs if recipe calls for sweet milk; reduce some other liquid from recipe

= 4 teaspoons quick-cooking tapioca

Baking Powder, 1 teaspoon single-acting

= $\frac{3}{4}$ teaspoon double-acting baking powder

❖ **Bananas** ❖

1 lb. = 3 to 4 whole

1 lb. = 2 cups, mashed

Barbecue Sauce

½ cup vinegar

1 cup ketchup

½ cup onion, chopped

½ teaspoon cayenne pepper

½ cup brown sugar

2 teaspoons dry mustard

2 tablespoons Worcestershire sauce

½ cup vegetable oil

½ teaspoon salt (optional)

2 tablespoons liquid smoke (optional)

Combine ingredients. Simmer for 30 minutes, if desired. Yields 2⅓ cups.

Basil, dried

= tarragon

= summer savory

Basmati Rice

= long-grain white rice

Bay Leaf

= thyme

❖ **Beans, dried** ❖

1 lb. = $1\frac{1}{2}$ to 2 cups

1 lb = 5 to 6 cups cooked

1 cup = 2 to $2\frac{1}{2}$ cups canned

Bean Sprouts

= celery

See Sprouts

Beef, ground

= ground turkey

= ground pork

= ground veal

= ground lamb

Note: Combinations of beef and these substitutes can also be used in most recipes.

Beet Greens

See Greens

Belgian Endive

= fennel

See Lettuce

Bermuda Onions

See Onions

Blackberries

= boysenberries

= loganberries

= raspberries

Black Pepper

= allspice in cooking, especially if salt is used in dish

Black Peppercorns

= white peppercorns

Note: Peppercorns vary in strength.

Blueberries

= huckleberries

= elderberries

Bok Choy or Chinese Cabbage

= Napa cabbage

= savoy cabbage

= green cabbage

Borage

= cucumber, especially in dishes with yogurt

Bouquet Garni

= 3 sprigs parsley, 1 sprig thyme, 1 bay leaf.
   (*Optional:* basil, celery leaf, fennel, marjoram,
   tarragon, and other similar aromatic herbs)

Bourbon
= whiskey

Boysenberries
= blackberries

= raspberries

Brandy
= cognac

= rum

❖ Bread ❖

1 lb. = 10 to 14 slices

1 slice = $\frac{1}{2}$ cup soft bread crumbs

1 slice = $\frac{1}{4}$ to $\frac{1}{3}$ cup dry bread crumbs

---

Bread Crumbs, dry, $\frac{1}{4}$ cup
= $\frac{1}{4}$ cup cracker crumbs

= $\frac{1}{2}$ slice bread, cubed, toasted, and crumbled

= $\frac{1}{4}$ cup rolled oats

= $\frac{1}{3}$ cup soft bread crumbs

= $\frac{1}{4}$ cup matzoh meal

= $\frac{1}{4}$ cup flour

= $\frac{1}{4}$ cup crushed corn flakes

Broccoli rabe or Italian turnip
See Greens

Broth, Beef, 1 cup

= 1 bouillon cube plus 1 cup water

= 1 cup beef stock

= 1 cup beef consommé

Broth, Chicken, 1 cup

= 1 bouillon cube plus 1 cup water

= 1 cup chicken stock

Bulgur

= cracked wheat

= buckwheat or kasha

= brown rice

= couscous

= millet

= quinoa

Butter, for frying

= oil

= bacon grease (this will flavor food, too)

Butter, in baking

= margarine

= shortening

Note: Oil is generally not interchangeable with butter in baking.

Butter, 1 cup

= 1 cup margarine

= $7/8$ cup vegetable shortening

= $7/8$ cup lard

Butter, 1 cup, *continued*

= $7/8$ cup cottonseed oil

= $7/8$ cup nut oil

= $7/8$ cup corn oil

= $2/3$ cup chicken fat (not for baking or sweets)

= $7/8$ cup solid shortening

Note: For softened butter, or to stretch butter, blend $1/2$ cup corn oil or safflower oil into 1 lb. butter; refrigerate.

❖ Butter ❖

1 lb. = 4 sticks

1 lb. = 2 cups

1 cup = 2 sticks

1 stick = $1/2$ cup

2 tablespoons = $1/4$ stick

2 tablespoons = 1 ounce

4 tablespoons = $1/2$ stick

4 tablespoons = 2 ounces

8 tablespoons = 1 stick

8 tablespoons = 4 ounces

16 tablespoons = 2 sticks

16 tablespoons = 8 ounces

Buttermilk

= 1 cup milk plus $1\frac{3}{4}$ tablespoons cream of tartar

= sour cream

Butternut Squash

= acorn squash

= pumpkin

= buttercup squash

C

Cabbage

See Chinese Cabbage, Green Cabbage, Red Cabbage, Savoy Cabbage

---

❖ Cabbage ❖

1 lb. = 4 cups shredded raw

1 lb. = 2 cups cooked

Cactus or Nopal

= green pepper

= okra

Cactus Pear

= kiwi

= watermelon

Capers

= pickled, green nasturtium seeds

= chopped green olives

Capon

= large roasting chicken

Caraway Seed

= fennel seed

= cumin seed

Cardamom

= cinnamon

= mace

Carrots

= parsnips

❖ Carrots ❖

1 lb. = 3 cups shredded or sliced raw

Cauliflower

= kohlrabi

Cayenne Pepper

= hot red pepper, ground

= chili powder

Celery

= green pepper

= jicama

= bean sprouts

= Belgian endive

= fennel

❖ Celery ❖

1 stalk = $\frac{1}{3}$ cup diced

Celery Root or Celeriac

= kohlrabi

= turnip

Celery Seed

= dill seed

Cèpe (Porcini or Boletus) Mushrooms

= Shiitake mushrooms

See Mushrooms

Chanterelle Mushrooms

= pied de mouton or hedgehog mushrooms

See Mushrooms

Chard

See Greens

Chayote Squash or Mirliton or Christophine Squash

= green peppers, when cooked and stuffed

= large zucchini, cooked

❖ Cheese ❖

4 ounces = 1 cup shredded

Cheese— *Within each group, these cheeses can be substituted for each other.*

= fontina
= Havarti
= Monterey Jack
= muenster
= Port-Salut

= American
= cheddar
= colby
= longhorn

= Edam
= Gouda

= Emmenthaler
= Gruyère

= Jarlsberg
= raclette
= Swiss

= mozzarella [not buffalo mozzarella] (for cooking)
= provolone

= bleu (blue) cheese
= Roquefort

= Brie
= Camenbert

= Gorgonzola
= Stilton

= Parmesan
= pecorino
= Romano

= buffalo milk mozzarella
= mozzarella (not for cooking)

= chèvre or goat (white)
= feta

= cottage cheese
= cream cheese
= farmer cheese
= hoop cheese

= mascarpone

= ricotta

= yogurt (especially in dips)

Cherimoya

= a mixture of pears, pineapple, and banana with lemon/lime juice

Chervil

= parsley

= tarragon (use less)

= anise (use less)

= Italian parsley

See Lettuce

Chicken, pieces

= turkey

= Cornish game hen

= rabbit

Chicken Breasts, boneless

= turkey breast slices

= veal scallops

Chile (or Chili) Oil or Red Pepper Oil

3 tablespoons sesame oil

3 to 4 spicy red peppers

Heat oil. Fry peppers until they turn dark. Remove peppers and discard. Use the remaining oil.

Chile or Chili Peppers, hot

= habanero

= Fresno

= jalapeño

= serrano

Chile or Chili Peppers, milder

= Anaheim or chile verde

= banana peppers or Hungarian wax peppers

= pepperoncini

= poblano (called ancho when dried)

Note: Chili peppers vary greatly in strength from mild to extra-hot, so use care when attempting substitutions.

Chili Powder

= cayenne pepper (*Optional:* add cumin, oregano, garlic, and other spices)

Chinese Cabbage

= cabbage

= lettuce

Chinese Parsley

See Cilantro

Chives

= green onion tops

= onion powder (use small amount)

= leeks

= shallots (use less)

21

❖ Baking Chocolate ❖

1 square = 1 ounce

Chocolate, Baking, unsweetened, 1 ounce or square

= 3 tablespoons unsweetened cocoa plus 1 tablespoon butter or margarine

= 3 tablespoons carob powder plus 2 tablespoons water

Chocolate, Baking, unsweetened pre-melted, 1 ounce

= 3 tablespoons unsweetened cocoa plus 1 tablespoon oil or melted shortening

Chocolate, Semi-sweet, 6 ounces chips, bits, or squares

= 9 tablespoons cocoa plus 7 tablespoons sugar plus 3 tablespoons butter or margarine

Chocolate, White

Note: There is no exact substitute for white chocolate.

Chocolate, White, chips

= semi-sweet or milk chocolate chips, in cookies or cakes

❖ Chocolate Chips ❖

1 12-ounce package = 2 cups

Chutney

1 8-ounce jar apricot or peach preserves

1 clove garlic, minced, or 1/2 teaspoon garlic powder

1/2 teaspoon powdered ginger, or 1 tablespoon fresh or candied ginger

1/2 teaspoon salt

1 tablespoon apple cider vinegar

1/2 cup raisins (optional)

Combine ingredients. Yields 1 1/2 cups.

Cilantro or Coriander Leaf or Chinese Parsley

- = parsley and lemon juice
- = Italian parsley (for looks)
- = orange peel with a little sage
- = lemon grass with a little mint

Cinnamon

- = allspice (use less)
- = cardamom

Clementines

- = tangerines
- = mandarin oranges

Cloves, ground

= allspice

= nutmeg

= mace

Club Soda

= mineral water

= seltzer

Cockles

= small clams

Cocktail Sauce

2 tablespoons horseradish

$\frac{1}{2}$ cup ketchup

1$\frac{1}{2}$ teaspoons Worcestershire sauce (optional)

2 tablespoons lemon juice (optional)

black pepper (optional)

bottled hot sauce (to taste; optional)

$\frac{1}{2}$ cup chili sauce (optional)

Combine ingredients.

Coconut, grated

Note: If less than ½ cup, can be omitted from recipe.

Coconut Milk, fresh, thick, 1 cup

= 4 to 5 tablespoons coconut cream, solidified, dissolved in 1 cup hot water or milk

= 1 cup top layer of canned cream of coconut liquid

= 1 cup medium cream with 1 teaspoon coconut flavoring

Coconut Milk, fresh, thin, 1 cup

= 2 tablespoons coconut cream, solidified, dissolved in 1 cup hot water or milk

= 1 cup canned cream of coconut liquid

= 1 cup whole milk with 1 teaspoon coconut flavoring

= 1 cup milk beaten with 3 tablespoons grated coconut

❖ Coffee ❖

½ cup strong brewed = 1 teaspoon instant in ½ cup water

1 lb. ground = 80 tablespoons

1 lb. ground = 30–40 cups (servings)

Cognac

= brandy

Collard Greens

See Greens

Coriander Leaf

See Cilantro

Coriander Seed, ground

= caraway plus cumin

= lemon plus sage

❖ Corn ❖

6 ears = 2 to 3 cups kernels

Corn Flour

= flour, up to a few tablespoons, for thickening

See Flour

Cornish Game Hen

= squab

= quail

Cornmeal

= (corn) grits

= polenta

Cornstarch

= flour, up to a few tablespoons, for thickening

See Flour

Corn Syrup, light, 1 cup
= 1¼ cups sugar plus ⅓ cup liquid, boiled together till syrupy

---

❖ Cottage Cheese ❖
1 lb. = 2 cups

Cottage Cheese
See Cheese, Cottage

Couscous
= bulgur (cracked wheat)

= quinoa

= kasha

= millet

= orzo

= rice

Crayfish
= small lobster

= prawns

= langouste (langoustine)

Cream, Clotted
= heavy cream, whipped to soft peaks

= sour cream with a pinch of baking soda

= crème fraiche

Cream, Heavy, not for whipping, 1 cup

= ¾ cup milk plus ¼ cup shortening or butter

= ⅔ cup evaporated milk

❖ Heavy or Whipping Cream ❖

1 cup = 2 cups whipped

Cream, Light (or Half and Half), 1 cup

= ½ cup heavy cream plus ½ cup milk

= ⅞ cup milk plus 3 tablespoons butter or margarine

= ½ cup evaporated milk plus ½ cup milk

Cream, Whipped, sweetened, 1 cup

= 1 4-ounce package frozen whipped cream topping

= 1 envelope whipped topping mix, prepared as directed

= 1 mashed banana beaten with 1 stiffly beaten egg white plus 1 teaspoon sugar

= 1 cup nonfat dry milk powder whipped with 1 cup ice water and sweetened to taste (this is for low-calorie desserts and drinks; it will not hold firm)

= ice-cold evaporated milk, whipped (use immediately)

Cream Cheese

= cottage cheese blended with cream or cream with a little butter and/or milk to correct consistency

Crème Fraiche

= sour cream, in recipes

= $\frac{1}{2}$ sour cream and $\frac{1}{2}$ heavy cream

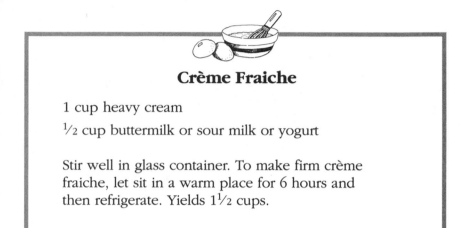

Crème Fraiche

1 cup heavy cream

$\frac{1}{2}$ cup buttermilk or sour milk or yogurt

Stir well in glass container. To make firm crème fraiche, let sit in a warm place for 6 hours and then refrigerate. Yields $1\frac{1}{2}$ cups.

Cumin

= $\frac{1}{3}$ anise plus $\frac{2}{3}$ caraway

= fennel

Currants

= gooseberries

Currants, 1 cup (dried)

= 1 cup raisins

= 1 cup soft prunes or dates, finely chopped

Note: If less than $\frac{1}{2}$ cup, can be omitted from recipe.

Curry Powder

2 tablespoons ground coriander

1 tablespoon black pepper

2 tablespoons cumin

2 tablespoons red pepper

2 tablespooons turmeric

2 tablespoons ground ginger

Optional: allspice, cinnamon, ground fennel, fenugreek, garlic powder, mace

Combine. Yields ⅔ cup.

D

Daikon

= jicama

= radish

Dandelion Greens

See Greens

See Lettuce

❖ Dates ❖

1 lb. = 2⅔ cups chopped, pitted

Dates

= raisins

= figs

= prunes

Note: If less than ½ cup, can be omitted from recipe.

Dill Seed

= caraway

= celery seed

E

Edible Blossoms, for garnish and in salads

= bachelor buttons

= blue borage

= calendula petals

= chive blossoms

= Johnny-jump-ups

= mini carnations

= nasturtiums

= pansies

= rocket

= rose petals

= snap dragons

= violets

= wild radish

❖ Eggs ❖

1 cup = 4 to 5 large

1 cup = 8 to 10 whites

1 cup = 10 to 12 yolks

32

Eggs, for scrambling

= tofu, lightly chopped

Eggs, Whole

= 2 tablespoons liquid plus 2 tablespoons flour plus ½ table-spoon shortening plus ½ teaspoon baking powder

= 2 yolks plus 1 tablespoon water

= 2 yolks, in custards, sauces, or similar mixtures

= 2 tablespoons oil plus 1 tablespoon water

= 1 teaspoon cornstarch plus 3 tablespoons more liquid in recipe

Note: If halving recipe, do not try to halve one egg; use one whole egg.

If short one *more* egg in recipe, substitute 1 teaspoon vinegar or 1 teaspoon baking powder.

Elderberries

= blueberries

= huckleberries

Elephant Garlic

= garlic (use less)

Endive or Curly Endive

= Belgian endive

= chicory

= escarole

See Lettuce

Enoki (Enokitake) Mushrooms

= oyster mushrooms

See Mushrooms

Escarole

= arugula

= endive

Evaporated Milk

= light cream or half and half

= heavy cream

F

Fava Beans

= lima beans, especially baby lima beans

Feijoa

See Guava

Fennel, bulb or Florentine

= Belgian endive

= celery

Fennel Seed

= anise seed or star anise

= caraway seed

❖ Figs ❖

1 lb. = 2⅔ cups chopped

Figs

Note: If less than ½ cup, can be omitted from recipe.

Filé Powder

See Gumbo Filé

Fines Herbes

Equal amounts of parsley, tarragon, chervil, and chives

Fish Fillets

= bass or sea bass, also known as Mexican bass or Chilean bass

= bluefish

= carp

= catfish

= cod

= coho salmon, also known as salmon trout

= flounder

= grouper

= haddock

Fish Fillets, *continued*

= halibut

= ling cod

= John Dory

= mahimahi

= monkfish, also known as lotte

= muskellunge, also known as muskie

= nilefish

= orange roughy

= pickerel

= pike

= plaice

= pollock

= red snapper

= rock cod

= rockfish

= salmon

= sandab

= scrod (this is a type of catch, not a type of fish)

= shark (dogfish)

= sole

= striped bass

= talapia, also known as golden talapia or St. Peter's fish

= trout

= turbot

= walleyed pike

= whitefish

Fish Steaks

- = ahi
- = albacore
- = cod
- = halibut
- = John Dory
- = mackerel
- = ono
- = salmon
- = sea bass
- = shark
- = swordfish
- = tuna

Fish, Whole

- = bass
- = catfish
- = flounder
- = halibut
- = mackerel
- = muskellunge
- = perch
- = pike
- = salmon
- = smelt
- = trout
- = turbot

Five Spice Powder, for Oriental cooking

Equal amounts of anise, fennel, cinnamon, black pepper, and cloves

Flavorings (extracts and aromatics)

Commonly available; some are imitation:

almond

anise

banana

brandy

butter

cherry

chocolate

coconut

lemon

liquid smoke

maple

orange

peppermint

pineapple

root beer

rose water

rum

vanilla

See Liqueurs

❖ Flour ❖

1 lb. white = $3\frac{1}{2}$ to 4 cups

1 cup white = 1 cup plus 2 tablespoons cake flour

1 lb. cake = 4 to $4\frac{1}{2}$ cups

1 cup cake = $\frac{7}{8}$ cup white flour

1 lb. whole wheat = 3 cups sifted

Flour, for thickening, up to a few tablespoons only

= Bisquick

= tapioca, quick cooking

= cornstarch or corn flour (use less)

= arrowroot (use less)

= brown rice flour or soy flour or rye flour

= potato starch or potato flour

= mashed potatoes, flakes or prepared

= 1 whole egg or 2 yolks or 2 whites (especially for cooked sauces)—whisk continuously

= pancake mix, for frying pork chops or chicken

Flour, Graham

= whole wheat flour

Flour, Self-rising, 1 cup

= 1 cup flour plus $\frac{1}{4}$ teaspoon baking powder
(*Optional:* add a pinch of salt)

Flour, White, for baking, 1 cup

= 1 cup plus 2 tablespoons cake flour

= $\frac{3}{4}$ cup whole wheat flour; reduce shortening to $\frac{2}{3}$ the amount for cookies; add 1 or 2 more tablespoons liquid for cakes; add more for bread.

Note: Whole wheat flour will make the product denser (heavier); it's advisable to start out substituting half whole wheat or other grain flours. Rye, for instance, has a nutty flavor. Soy can also be used for extra protein; substitute $\frac{1}{10}$ to $\frac{1}{4}$ soy flour for wheat flour.

Flour, Whole Wheat, 1 cup

= 1 cup graham flour

= 2 tablespoons wheat germ plus enough white flour to make 1 cup.

Note: Product may be less dense or lighter when using white flour.

Flowers

See Edible Blossoms

Focaccio Bread

= baked pizza dough

G

Galangal or Laos Powder

= ginger root or powdered ginger plus cardamom

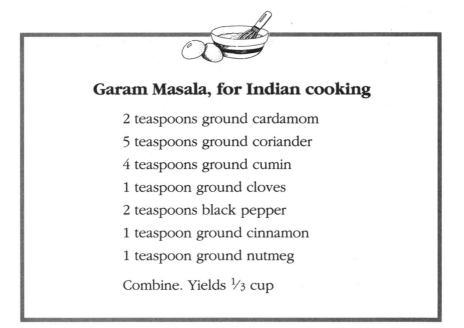

Garam Masala, for Indian cooking

2 teaspoons ground cardamom

5 teaspoons ground coriander

4 teaspoons ground cumin

1 teaspoon ground cloves

2 teaspoons black pepper

1 teaspoon ground cinnamon

1 teaspoon ground nutmeg

Combine. Yields $\frac{1}{3}$ cup

Garlic, 1 clove

= $\frac{1}{4}$ teaspoon minced, dried garlic

= $\frac{1}{8}$ teaspoon garlic powder

= $\frac{1}{4}$ teaspoon garlic juice

= $\frac{1}{2}$ teaspoon garlic salt (and omit $\frac{1}{2}$ teaspoon salt from recipe)

= garlic chives (use more)

= elephant garlic (use more)

❖ Garlic ❖

1 clove garlic = ½–1 teaspoon chopped garlic

Garlic Butter

1 clove garlic, mashed

4 tablespoons salted butter, creamed or melted

Combine. Yields ¼ cup.

Garlic, Green

= leeks

Ghee

= clarified butter

Ginger, fresh, grated

= powdered ginger (use less)

= minced, crystalized ginger with sugar washed off

Ginger, powdered

= ⅓ mace plus ⅔ lemon peel

Gooseberries

= currants

Green Beans

= haricots verts

= wax beans

Green Cabbage

= Savoy cabbage

= Chinese cabbage

= kohlrabi

= lettuce

Green Onions

= scallions

= leeks

= shallots (use less)

= chives

❖ Green Peppers ❖

1 large = 1 cup diced

Green Peppers

= yellow peppers

= red peppers

= celery

43

Greens, mild in flavor

= beet greens

= collard greens

= broccoli rabe, also known as rapini

Greens, medium in flavor

= kale

= spinach

= Swiss chard, also known as chard

Greens, strong in flavor

= dandelion greens

= mustard greens

= turnip greens

Grits (corn)

= cornmeal

= polenta

Guavas

= pears with nutmeg and lime juice

Gumbo Filé

= sassafras

H

Haricots Verts

= young green beans

Herb Butter

$\frac{1}{2}$ teaspoon parsley

$\frac{1}{2}$ teaspoon chives

$\frac{1}{2}$ teaspoon tarragon

$\frac{1}{2}$ teaspoon shallots

4 tablespoons salted butter, creamed

Combine. Yields $\frac{1}{3}$ cup.

❖ Honey ❖

1 lb. = $1\frac{1}{3}$ cups

Honey, in baking, 1 cup

= $1\frac{1}{4}$ cups sugar plus $\frac{1}{4}$ cup more liquid

Note: This may cause the product to brown faster and may necessitate a lower oven temperature.

Honey Butter

1 tablespoon honey

3 tablespoons unsalted butter, creamed

Combine. Yields ¼ cup.

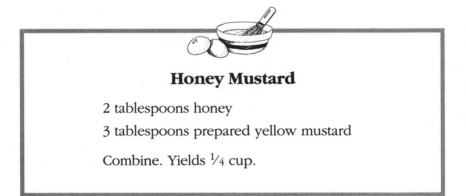

Honey Mustard

2 tablespoons honey

3 tablespoons prepared yellow mustard

Combine. Yields ¼ cup.

Hot Fudge Sauce

1 egg, slightly beaten

1 cup sugar

$\frac{1}{4}$ cup cream

2 squares unsweetened baking chocolate

1 tablespoon butter

1 teaspoon vanilla

Melt first 4 ingredients slowly over low heat. Bring to a boil. Cool a minute. Beat in butter and vanilla. Serve warm over ice cream. Yields $1\frac{1}{2}$ cups.

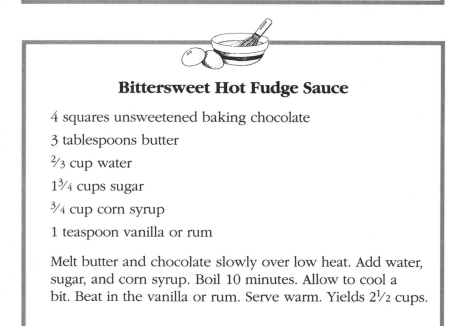

Bittersweet Hot Fudge Sauce

4 squares unsweetened baking chocolate

3 tablespoons butter

$\frac{2}{3}$ cup water

$1\frac{3}{4}$ cups sugar

$\frac{3}{4}$ cup corn syrup

1 teaspoon vanilla or rum

Melt butter and chocolate slowly over low heat. Add water, sugar, and corn syrup. Boil 10 minutes. Allow to cool a bit. Beat in the vanilla or rum. Serve warm. Yields $2\frac{1}{2}$ cups.

Hot Pepper Jelly

1 cup apple jelly

1½ small, hot chilies or 2 tablespoons canned chili peppers

Combine. Process in a food processor. Yields 1 cup.

Hot Pepper Sauce

= bottled hot sauce

= Tabasco sauce

= ground red pepper

= cayenne pepper

= hot red pepper flakes

= chili powder

Hot Red Pepper Flakes

= chopped, dried red pepper pods

= red pepper (use less)

Huckleberries

= blueberries

= elderberries

J

Japanese Pears

See Asian Pears

Jerusalem Artichoke or Sunchoke

= artichoke heart

Jicama

= daikon

= raw turnip

= water chestnut

Juniper Berries

= a dash of gin

K

Kabocha Squash

= buttercup squash

= butternut squash

Kale

See Greens

Ketchup

½ cup tomato sauce

2 tablespoons sugar

2 tablespoons vinegar

½ teaspoon salt

⅛ teaspoon ground cloves

or

½ cup tomato sauce

¼ cup sugar

2 tablespoons vinegar

1 teaspoon salt

Combine. Yields ¾ cup.

Kidney Beans

= pink beans

= pinto beans

= red beans

Note: These substitutes are smaller beans.

Kiwi Fruit

= strawberries with a little lime juice

Note: Use only fresh berries.

Kohlrabi

- = cauliflower
- = artichoke heart
- = broccoli stems
- = cabbage
- = celeriac
- = radish
- = turnip

L

Leeks

- = shallots
- = green onions
- = onions (use less)

❖ Lemon ❖

1 medium = 2 to 3 tablespoons juice

1 medium = 1 to 2 teaspoons rind, grated

Lemon

- = lime

Lemon, as flavoring

= lime

= lemongrass

= verbena

Lemongrass

= lemon or lemon rind

= verbena

Lemon Juice

= vinegar

= lime juice

= crushed Vitamin C pills mixed with water to taste (for small amounts)

Lemon Peel, grated

= equal amount of marmalade

= equal amount of lime or orange peel

Note: If less than 1 tablespoon, can be omitted from recipe, especially if another flavoring or essence is used.

See Flavorings

Lentils

= yellow split peas

Lettuce and Salad Greens, buttery and soft

= bibb, also known as limestone

= Boston, also known as butter

= mâche, also known as lamb's lettuce or corn salad

= oak leaf

= red salad bowl

Lettuce and Salad Greens, crisp and crunchy

- = cos
- = curly endive
- = iceberg
- = romaine
- = salad bowl

Lettuce and Salad Greens, pungent to slightly bitter

- = arugula, also known as rocket
- = Belgian endive
- = chervil
- = dandelion greens
- = escarole
- = lovage
- = mustard greens
- = pepper grass, also known as garden cress
- = radicchio, also known as chicory
- = sorrel
- = watercress

Lima Beans

- = fava beans

Lime

- = lemon

Lime Juice

- = lemon juice

Liqueurs

Standard liqueur flavors include:

Mint—Creme de Menthe

Orange—Curaçao, Grand Marnier, Cointreau

Raspberry—Cassis, Chambord

Anise (or licorice)—Pastis, Ouzo, Pernod, Arak

Note: One liqueur can be used in place of two in a recipe.

Loganberries

= blackberries

= boysenberries

= raspberries

Lovage

= celery leaves

See Lettuce

See Greens

Lychee

= peeled grapes

M

❖ Macaroni ❖

1 lb. elbow = 8 to 9 cups cooked

Macaroni

See Pasta

Mace

= allspice

= cloves

= nutmeg (*Optional:* add cardamom)

Mâche

See Lettuce

Madeira

= sherry

= port

Mango

= peach with a little lemon and allspice

❖ Margarine ❖

1 lb. = 4 sticks

1 lb. = 2 cups

1 stick = ½ cup

Margarine

= butter

= shortening

Note: See Butter entries.

Marinade for Beef, Lamb, or Chicken

1 cup red wine or red wine vinegar for beef or lamb; 1 cup dry white wine for chicken

1 cup salad oil or olive oil or combination

2 cloves garlic

1 teaspoon black pepper, freshly ground

1/4 cup minced fresh parsley

1/2 teaspoon dried thyme

1/2 teaspoon dried marjoram

1 bay leaf

Optional:

1 small onion, chopped

1 small carrot, chopped

2 allspice berries, whole

1 teaspoon salt

1/2 teaspoon dried rosemary

Combine ingredients. Yields 2 1/2 to 3 cups.

Marinade for Fish or Chicken

1½ cups soy sauce

1¾ cups ketchup

¼ cup dry red wine

2 tablespoons fresh grated ginger

2 tablespoons brown sugar

1 small onion, finely chopped

juice of 1 lemon (2 to 3 tablespoons)

dash of bottled hot sauce

2 cloves garlic, mashed

Combine ingredients. Yields 4¼ cups.

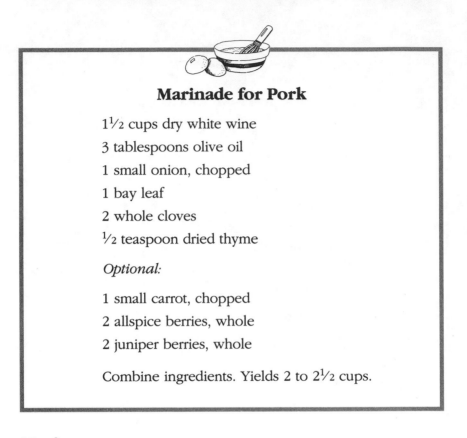

Marinade for Pork

1½ cups dry white wine

3 tablespoons olive oil

1 small onion, chopped

1 bay leaf

2 whole cloves

½ teaspoon dried thyme

Optional:

1 small carrot, chopped

2 allspice berries, whole

2 juniper berries, whole

Combine ingredients. Yields 2 to 2½ cups.

Marjoram

= oregano (use less)

= thyme

❖ Marshmallows ❖

1 large = 6 miniature

11 large = 1 cup

Masa Harina

= corn flour

Mascarpone

= cream cheese, whipped with a little butter and/or heavy cream

See Cheese, Mascarpone

Matsuke Mushrooms

= morel mushrooms

See Mushrooms

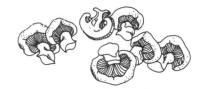

Maui Onions

See Onions, Sweet

Mayonnaise

= yogurt or sour cream, especially in small amounts and in dips

(*Optional:* add lemon juice)

Melon

= papaya

= mango

Melon, Crenshaw

= Spanish melon

Melon, Honeydew

= Casaba melon

Mexican Mint Marigold

= tarragon

Milk, Evaporated

= light cream or half and half

= heavy cream

Milk, in baking

= fruit juice plus ½ teaspoon baking soda added to the flour

Milk, 1 cup

= 1 cup light cream (*Optional:* delete up to 4 tablespoons shortening from recipe)

= ½ cup evaporated milk plus ½ cup water

= 1 cup skim milk (*Optional:* add 2 tablespoons shortening)

= 3 tablespoons powdered milk plus 1 cup water (add 2 tablespoons butter if whole milk is required)

= soy or nut milks, in recipes

Millet

= orzo (or other tiny pasta)

= barley

= quinoa

Mineral water

= club soda

= seltzer

Mint

= mint or spearmint tea from tea bags or bulk tea

= crème de menthe, in sweets

Mirin

= sweet sherry

= sweet vermouth

Mirliton

See Chayote

Molasses, in baking, 1 cup

= ¾ cup white or brown sugar plus ¼ cup liquid

Morel Mushrooms

= matsuke mushrooms

Mung Beans

= split peas

Mushrooms

See Cèpe, Chanterelle, Matsuke, Morel, Oyster, Pied de Mouton, Porcini, Shiitake

---

❖ Mushrooms, Fresh ❖

1 lb. = 5 cups sliced

1 lb. = 12 ounces canned, drained

Mustard, Dry, 1 teaspoon

= 1 tablespoon prepared mustard from jar

Mustard Greens

See Lettuce

See Greens

Mustard, Hot Chinese

= Coleman's English dry mustard, prepared with water

Prepared Mustard

1 teaspoon dry mustard

1/2 teaspoon water

2 drops vinegar

Combine well. Yields 1/2 tablespoon.

N

Nectarines

= peaches

❖ Noodles ❖

1 lb. dried = 6 to 8 cups cooked

Noodles

See Pasta

Nopal

See Cactus

Nutmeg

= allspice

= cloves

= mace

❖ Nuts ❖

1 lb. shelled = 4 cups nutmeats

1 lb. in shell = 1$\frac{2}{3}$ cups nutmeats

Nuts, in baking

= bran

= soy nuts, toasted and chopped

Note: If less than ½ cup, can be omitted from recipe.

O

Oil, for cooking, interchangeable:

= canola oil

= corn oil

= light sesame oil

= olive oil

= peanut oil (adds some flavor)

= rice bran oil

= safflower oil

= soy oil

= vegetable oil

Note: The burning temperatures of different oils, butter, and margarine vary.

Oil, for salads, flavored

= almond oil

= Asian sesame or dark sesame oil (mix with an unflavored oil)

= hazelnut oil

= olive oil (use virgin)

= walnut oil

Oil, for salads, unflavored, interchangeable

= avocado oil

= canola oil

= rice bran oil

= safflower oil

= soy oil

Oil, for sautéing (not for deep-fat frying)

= margarine or butter

Oil, in baking, 1 tablespoon

= 1¼ tablespoons butter

= 1¼ tablespoons margarine

= 1 tablespoon mayonnaise, in cake recipes

Note: Use these substitutions only for small amounts, up to a few tablespoons. If substituting olive or other strong oils in baking, add a few drops of mint to mask the pungency; the baked goods will have a mint flavor.

Okra

= eggplant (although texture will be different)

❖ Onion ❖

1 medium = ¾ cup chopped

Onion, White or Yellow, 1 medium or ¼ cup

= red onion, not usually used for cooking

= 1 tablespoon instant minced onion

Onion, White or Yellow, *continued*

= ¼ cup frozen chopped onion

= 1 tablespoon onion powder

= shallots (use more)

= leeks

= green onions (use more)

Onion Powder

See Onion, White or Yellow

Onions, Sweet

= Vidalia

= Walla Walla

= Maui

= red, also called Italian red or purple

= Bermuda

= Spanish yellow

Orange Peel

= tangerine peel

= marmalade

= Grand Marnier

= Curaçao

= Cointreau

= lemon or lime peel

Orange Peel, grated

= equal amount of marmalade

= equal amount of lemon or lime peel

Note: If less than 1 tablespoon, can be omitted from recipe.

❖ Oranges ❖

1 medium = $\frac{1}{3}$ to $\frac{1}{2}$ cup juice

1 medium = 1 to 2 tablespoons peel, grated

Oregano

= marjoram

= rosemary

= thyme, fresh

Oyster Mushrooms

= button or market mushrooms

P

Pancake Syrup

= fruit jelly, melted (add water to thin)

Pancetta

= lean bacon, cooked

= prosciutto

= thinly sliced ham

Paprika

= turmeric with red or cayenne pepper

Parsley

= chervil

= tarragon

Parsley Root

= parsnip

Parsnips

= parsley root

= carrots

Passion Fruit

= pomegranates with apricot and grapefruit

= pomegranates

Pasta, filled

= agnolotti

= ravioli

= tortellini

= cannelloni

= manicotti

Pasta, flat

= noodles

= fettuccine

= linguine

= tagliatelle

Pasta, medium

= rice noodles

= spaghetti

= soba (buck wheat) noodles

= Oriental (ramen) noodles

Pasta, miscellaneous shapes

= farfalle ("butterflies")

= mostaccioli ("little mustaches")

= rotelle ("wheels")

= rotini ("corkscrews")

= ruote ("wagon wheels")

= gnocchi (miniature potato dumplings)

Pasta, thin

= angel hair

= bucatini

= fedelini

= vermicelli

= fusilli

= spaghettini

= cappellini

Pasta, tiny

= orzo

= pastini

Pasta, tube

= bocconcini

= cannolicchi

= ditali

= macaroni

= penne

= rigatoni

= ziti

Pattypan Squash or Summer Squash

= yellow crookneck squash

= yellow straightneck squash

= zucchini

❖ Peaches ❖

1 lb. = 4 medium

1 lb. = 2 cups, sliced, peeled

Peaches

= nectarines

= cantaloupe (in an ice, primarily)

Peanut Butter

= sesame paste

= other nut butters

❖ **Peanuts** ❖

1 lb. shelled = 2 ¼ cups

Pear-Apple

See Asian Pears

Pears

= Asian pears

= apples

❖ **Peas** ❖

1 lb. in pod = 1 cup shelled

❖ **Pecans** ❖

1 lb. shelled = 3 to 4 cups nutmeats

Pecans

= walnuts, in small amounts

Pepper

See Black Pepper, Cayenne Pepper, Hot Red Pepper, Red Pepper

Peppercorns

See Black Peppercorns, White Peppercorns

Pepperoni

= sausage, cooked

= salami

Peppers

See Chile or Chili Peppers, Green Peppers, Red Peppers, Yellow Peppers

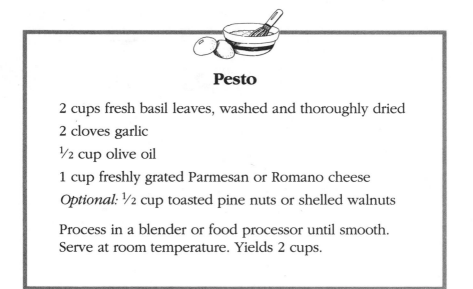

Pesto

2 cups fresh basil leaves, washed and thoroughly dried

2 cloves garlic

½ cup olive oil

1 cup freshly grated Parmesan or Romano cheese

Optional: ½ cup toasted pine nuts or shelled walnuts

Process in a blender or food processor until smooth. Serve at room temperature. Yields 2 cups.

Pickling Spice

4 3-inch cinnamon sticks

1 1-inch piece dried ginger root

2 tablespoons mustard seed

2 teaspoons whole allspice

2 teaspoons black peppercorns

2 teaspoons whole cloves

2 teaspoons dill seed

2 teaspoons coriander seed

2 teaspoons whole mace, crumbled

8 bay leaves, crumbled

1 whole 1$\frac{1}{2}$-inch dried red pepper, chopped

Combine ingredients. Yields $\frac{2}{3}$ cup.

Pied de Mouton or Hedgehog Mushrooms

= chanterelles

Pie Spice, Pumpkin or Apple

$\frac{1}{2}$ teaspoon cinnamon

$\frac{1}{4}$ teaspoon nutmeg

$\frac{1}{8}$ teaspoon allspice

$\frac{1}{8}$ teaspoon cardamom

$\frac{1}{4}$ teaspoon ground cloves

Combine spices. Yields enough for one 9-inch pie.

Pimento

= sweet red peppers, roasted and peeled

Pineapple guava

See Guava

Pine Nuts or Pignoli

= chopped walnuts for pesto and other Mediterranean-type recipes

= blanched, peeled, slivered almonds

Pink Beans

= pinto beans

= red beans

= kidney beans (these are larger)

Pinto Beans

= pink beans

= red beans

= kidney beans (these are larger)

Pita Bread

= flour tortillas

Polenta

= cornmeal

= grits

Ponzu Sauce

2 parts soy sauce

1 part lemon juice

Combine.

Porcini Mushrooms

= shiitake mushrooms

= cèpe or boletus mushrooms

Pork, ground

= sausage meat (omit salt and other spices from recipe)

Pork Fat, fresh

= salt pork, boiled briefly (omit salt from recipe)

= unsmoked bacon, boiled briefly (omit salt from recipe)

Port

= Madeira

= sherry

❖ Potatoes ❖

1 lb. = 3 medium

1 lb. = 3 cups sliced

1 lb. = 2¼ cups cooked

1 lb. = 1¾ cups mashed

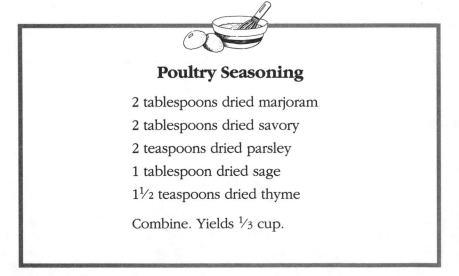

Poultry Seasoning

2 tablespoons dried marjoram

2 tablespoons dried savory

2 teaspoons dried parsley

1 tablespoon dried sage

1½ teaspoons dried thyme

Combine. Yields ⅓ cup.

Prawns

= shrimp

Prosciutto

= smoked ham

Prunes

= dates

= raisins

= dried apricots

Note: If less than 1/4 cup, can be omitted from recipe.

Pumpkin

= acorn squash

= butternut squash

❖ Prunes ❖

1 lb. = $2\frac{1}{4}$ cups pitted

Q

Quail

= Cornish game hen

= squab

Quince

= golden delicious apples

= Bartlett pears

Quinoa

= couscous

= millet

See Rice

R

Rabbit

= chicken pieces

Radicchio

See Lettuce

❖ Raisins ❖

1 lb. = $2\frac{3}{4}$ cups

Raisins, 1 cup

= 1 cup currants

= 1 cup soft prunes or dates, finely chopped

Note: If less than $\frac{1}{4}$ cup, can be omitted from recipe.

Rapini

See Greens

Raspberries

= blackberries

= boysenberries

Red Beans

= pinto beans

= pink beans

= kidney beans (these are larger)

Red Cabbage

= green cabbage

Red Onion

= Bermuda onion

= Maui onion

= Vidalia onion

See Onions, Sweet

Red Pepper, ground

= cayenne pepper

= chili powder

= hot pepper sauce

= bottled hot sauce

= hot red pepper flakes

Red Pepper Flakes, Hot

= chopped, dried red pepper pods

= red pepper (use less)

Red Pepper Oil

See Chile (or Chili) Oil

Red Pepper Sauce, Hot

See Hot Pepper Sauce

Red Peppers, Sweet

= green pepper

= yellow pepper

Note: This is for bell peppers, not chile or chili peppers.

❖ Rice ❖

1 cup uncooked = 3 cups cooked

1 lb. = 2 to 2½ cups uncooked

Rice

The following grains may be served instead of rice—or rice can be substituted for them

= barley

= bulgur

= couscous

= millet

= quinoa

Rice, "risotto" or arborio
- = short-grain white rice
- = short-grain brown rice

Seasoned Rice Vinegar

3 tablespoons white wine vinegar

1 tablespoon sugar

$\frac{1}{2}$ teaspoon salt

Combine. Yields $\frac{1}{4}$ cup.

Rice Wine
See Sake

Rocket
See Arugula

Romaine
See Lettuce

Rosemary
- = marjoram
- = oregano

Rum
- = brandy
- = cognac

S

Safflower or Azafran

= saffron (use only a tiny bit)

Saffron, ⅛ teaspoon

= 1 teaspoon dried yellow marigold petals

= 1 teaspoon azafran or safflower

= ½–1 teaspoon achiote seeds

= ½–1 teaspoon turmeric (for color)

Sage

= rosemary

= oregano

Sake

= very dry sherry or vermouth

= jui or Chinese rice wine

Salami

= pepperoni

Salsa

4 tomatoes, fresh or canned, chopped

$^1/_2$ cup green or red onions, chopped

$^1/_4$ cup cilantro, chopped

2 cloves garlic, minced

1 teaspoon salt

1 small jalapeño pepper, seeded and chopped

2 tablespoons lime juice or red wine vinegar

1 teaspoon olive oil

Combine all ingredients. Makes $1^1/_2$ to 2 cups.

Salt, as a flavor enhancer

= black pepper

= garlic

= onion powder

= mustard powder

= paprika

= red pepper

= lemon juice

= vinegar

= wine (not cooking wines)

Salt, Kosher

= table salt (use less)

Salt, Seasoned

1 cup salt

2½ teaspoons paprika

2 teaspoons dry mustard

1½ teaspoons oregano

1 teaspoon garlic powder

1 teaspoon onion powder

or:

½ cup salt

1 teaspoon paprika

1 teaspoon dry mustard

1 teaspoon garlic powder

½ teaspoon onion powder

Combine.

Sapote

= mango with vanilla or vanilla custard

= a mixture of peaches, lemon, and vanilla custard

Sardines, processed
- = small herring
- = small mackerel

Sassafras
- = gumbo filé

Sausage
- = pepperoni
- = ground pork with sage, marjoram, garlic, and onions to taste

Savory
- = thyme (*Optional:* add sage)

Scallions
- = green onions
- = shallots
- = leeks
- = onions (use less)

Scallops
- = shark

Seltzer
See Club Soda

Semolina
- = farina or similar breakfast cereal
- = cream of wheat

Sesame Seed

= finely chopped almonds

Shallots

= green onions

= leeks

= onions (use less)

= scallions (use more)

Sherry

= Madeira

= port

Shiitake Mushrooms

= porcini mushrooms (cèpe or boletus)

= meat, especially steak or veal

Shortening

See Butter or Margarine

Shortening, in baking, 1 cup

= 1 cup butter

= 1 cup margarine

Shrimp

= prawns

Snow Peas

= sugar snap peas

Sorrel

= spinach (add lemon)

See Lettuce

Sour Cream, 1 cup

= 1 tablespoon white vinegar plus enough milk to make 1 cup; let stand 5 minutes before using

= 1 tablespoon lemon juice plus enough evaporated milk to make 1 cup

= 1 cup plain yogurt, especially in dips and cold soups

= cottage cheese, mixed with yogurt, if desired, and 2 tablespoons milk and 1 tablespoon lemon juice; blend well

= 6 ounces cream cheese plus 3 tablespoons milk

= $\frac{1}{3}$ cup melted butter plus $\frac{3}{4}$ cup sour milk, for baking

Sour Milk, 1 cup

= $1\frac{1}{2}$ tablespoons lemon juice or vinegar plus enough milk to make 1 cup

Note: With pasteurized milk, this is the only way to make sour milk. Pasteurized milk will spoil, but it will not go sour like raw milk.

Soursops

= guavas and peaches

= melons and peaches

Soy Sauce

3 tablespoons Worcestershire sauce

1 tablespoon water

Combine. Yields ¼ cup.

Note: Light and dark soy sauce can be substituted for each other.

Indonesian-style Soy Sauce

½ cup soy sauce

¼ cup dark brown sugar

3 tablespoons dark corn syrup

1 tablespoon molasses

Combine. Makes ¾ cup.

❖ **Spaghetti** ❖

1 lb. = 6½ cups cooked

Spaghetti

See Pasta

❖ **Spinach** ❖

1 lb. fresh = 2 cups cooked

Spinach

See Greens

Split Peas

= mung beans, in salads

= lentils, in soups or stews

Sprouts

The following sprouts are interchangeable:

= alfalfa

= bean

= buckwheat

= sunflower

Note: Radish sprouts are spicy.

Squab

- = Cornish game hen
- = chicken halves
- = grouse
- = pigeon
- = quail

Squash

See Summer Squash, Winter Squash, and individual varieties

Star Anise or Anise Seed

- = fennel seed

Starfruit or Carambola

- = watermelon with lemon juice

Stock, Chicken, Beef, Veal, Fish

- = bouillon
- = consommé

Note: Stock in a sauce may be replaced by wine for up to ⅓ of stock required.

❖ Sugar ❖

Granulated white, 1 lb. = 2 cups

Powdered or confectioners, 1 lb. = 3½ to 4 cups

Firmly packed brown, 1 lb. = 2¼ cups

Sugar, Brown, in baking, $\frac{1}{2}$ cup

= $\frac{1}{2}$ cup white sugar plus 2 tablespoons molasses.

Note: To replace a combination of brown sugar and milk, use honey or molasses with powdered milk.

Sugar, Granulated White, in baking, 1 cup

= 1 cup superfine sugar

= 1 cup turbinado sugar

= 1 cup firmly packed brown sugar

= 2 cups powdered sugar, sifted

= $\frac{3}{4}$ cup honey or $1\frac{1}{4}$ cups molasses and reduce other liquid in recipe by $\frac{1}{4}$ cup; or add $\frac{1}{4}$ cup flour if no other liquid is called for

= 1 cup corn syrup, but never replace more than half the amount of sugar this way; always reduce the other liquid in the recipe by $\frac{1}{4}$ cup for each 2 cups sugar substituted this way

Notes:

• Sugar generally may be reduced by a quarter of the amount.

• Sugar can be reduced by $\frac{1}{2}$ cup if liquid is reduced by $\frac{1}{4}$ cup.

• A few tablespoons of granulated sugar may be replaced by maple sugar.

• Sugar substitutions tend to make baked goods heavier.

• Write to manufacturers of artificial sweeteners for recipes using those products.

Sugar, Superfine

= granulated sugar

Note: Granulated sugar may take longer to dissolve.

Sugar Snap Peas

= snow peas

Sumac

= lemongrass

= lemon

Summer Savory

= thyme (*Optional:* add sage)

Summer Squash or Pattypan Squash

= yellow crookneck squash

= yellow straightneck squash

= zucchini

Sunchokes

See Jerusalem Artichokes

Sunflower Sprouts

= watercress

See Sprouts

Sweet Potatoes

= yams

Swiss Chard

See Greens

T

Tahini

= ground sesame seeds

Tamarind

= dried apricots and dates

= chopped prunes and lemon juice

Tamarind, pods

= lemon juice

Tarragon

= anise (use less)

= Mexican mint marigold

= chervil (use more)

= parsley (use more)

Tartar Sauce

2 tablespoons pickle relish or pickles, chopped

6 tablespoons mayonnaise

1 tablespoon onion, chopped (optional)

1 tablespoon hard-boiled egg, chopped (optional)

a few drops lemon juice (optional)

Combine. Makes ½ cup.

❖ Tea ❖

1 lb. leaves = 100 servings

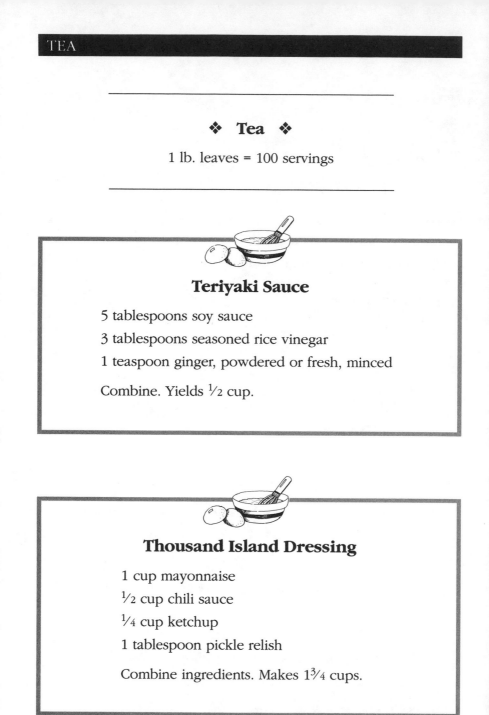

Teriyaki Sauce

5 tablespoons soy sauce

3 tablespoons seasoned rice vinegar

1 teaspoon ginger, powdered or fresh, minced

Combine. Yields ½ cup.

Thousand Island Dressing

1 cup mayonnaise

½ cup chili sauce

¼ cup ketchup

1 tablespoon pickle relish

Combine ingredients. Makes 1¾ cups.

Thyme

- = marjoram
- = oregano
- = savory
- = bay leaf

Tomatillos

- = fresh green tomatoes plus lemon juice
- = pickled green tomatoes

❖ Tomatoes ❖

1 lb. = 2 to 3 medium

1 lb. = 1 8-ounce can

1 lb. = 1 cup chopped

Tomatoes, canned, 1 cup

- = 1⅓ cups chopped fresh tomatoes, simmered

Tomatoes, cooked, seasoned, 1 lb.

- = 8 ounces tomato sauce, for cooking

Tomato Juice, 1 cup

- = 2 or 3 fresh, ripe tomatoes, peeled, seeded, and blended in blender or food processor (add salt and lemon juice to taste)
- = ½ cup tomato sauce plus ½ cup water

Tomato Paste, 1 tablespoon

= 1 tablespoon ketchup

= ½ cup tomato sauce (and reduce some other liquid from recipe)

Tomato Purée, 1 cup

= 1 cup tomato sauce

= ½ cup tomato paste plus ½ cup water

Tomato Sauce, 2 cups

= ¾ cup tomato paste plus 1 cup water

= 2 cups tomato purée

Tortillas

= pita bread, split

Triticale, flaked

= rolled oats

Triticale Berries

= wheat berries

Truffles, fresh

= canned truffles or canned truffle peels; add canning liquid

Note: The above substitution is nowhere near the fresh. Truffles are in season in the fall.

Turmeric

= mustard powder (*Optional:* add saffron)

Tuna, canned

= albacore

= cooked, boned chicken

Turnips, for cooking

= kohlrabi

= rutabaga

Turnips, raw

= jicama

= radish

Turnip Greens

See Greens

Twentieth Century Pears

See Asian Pears

U

Ugli or Ugli Fruit

= grapefruit plus sugar

V

Vanilla Extract, in baking

= almond extract

= peppermint or other extracts, which will alter the flavor of the products

Veal, scallops

= boned, skinned chicken breasts

= turkey breast slices

Verbena

= lemon peel

= lemongrass

Vermicelli

See Pasta

Vidalia Onions

See Onions, Sweet

Vienna sausages

= frankfurters

Vinegar

= lemon juice, in cooking and salads

= grapefruit juice, in salads

= wine, in marinades

Vinegar, Apple Cider

= champagne vinegar

= malt vinegar

Vinegar, Balsamic

= sherry vinegar

Vinegar, Champagne

= apple cider vinegar

Vinegar, Malt

= apple cider vinegar

Vinegar, Red Wine

= white wine vinegar

Vinegar, Sherry

= balsamic vinegar

Vinegar, White Wine

= red wine vinegar

Walla Walla Onions

See Onions, Sweet

Wasabi

= hot mustard powder mixed with a little water

Water Chestnuts

= jicama, raw

Watercress

= sunflower sprouts

See Lettuce

Wax Beans

= green beans

Whiskey

= bourbon

White Beans

= pea beans

= navy beans

White Peppercorns

= black peppercorns

Note: Peppercorns vary in strength.

Wine, for marinades, ½ cup

= ¼ cup vinegar plus 1 tablespoon sugar plus ¼ cup water

Winter Squash
- = acorn squash
- = butternut squash
- = dumpling squash
- = gold nugget squash
- = kabocha squash
- = pumpkin
- = table queen squash
- = turban squash

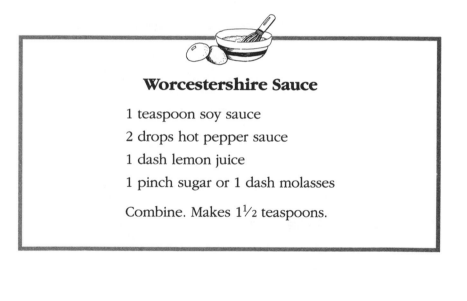

Worcestershire Sauce

1 teaspoon soy sauce

2 drops hot pepper sauce

1 dash lemon juice

1 pinch sugar or 1 dash molasses

Combine. Makes 1½ teaspoons.

Y

Yams

= sweet potatoes

❖ Yeast, Compressed, 1 cake ❖

= 2 envelopes dry yeast

= 2 tablespoons powdered yeast

❖ Yeast, Dry, 1 envelope ❖

= 1 tablespoon powdered yeast

= $\frac{1}{2}$ cake compressed yeast, crumbled

Yellow Finn Potatoes

= 2 parts white potatoes plus 1 part yams or sweet potatoes

Yellow or Gold Peppers

= red peppers

= green peppers

Yellow Squash, Crookneck or Straightneck

= pattypan squash

= zucchini

Yogurt, Plain

- = sour cream
- = crème fraiche
- = buttermilk
- = heavy cream
- = mayonnaise (in small amounts, especially in salads or dips)

Z

Zucchini

- = pattypan squash
- = yellow crookneck squash
- = yellow straightneck squash

Too Much

Sometimes, instead of not having a particular ingredient at all, you have the opposite problem: You end up with too much of something. The following is designed to remedy common kitchen disasters of this type.

Alcohol

If too much in punch or other mixed alcoholic drinks, float thin slices of cucumber to absorb the taste of alcohol.

Fat, in stew, soup, or gravy

Drop in ice cubes; the grease will stick to them. Remove quickly.

or

Wrap ice cubes in paper towels and draw over the surface. The fat will begin to solidify and stick to the paper towel. Repeat until enough fat is removed.

or

Place paper towel lightly on surface and allow to absorb fat, then remove. Repeat as necessary.

or

Use a flat lettuce leaf the same way.

or

Refrigerate dish. When cool, skim solidified fat from the top surface. Continue with recipe.

Garlic

Simmer a sprig or small bunch of parsley in stew or soup for ten minutes.

To remove onion and garlic flavors from hands, pots and pans, chopping boards, etc., rub with salt, lemon juice, or vinegar.

Ketchup, in a sauce

Add lemon juice to mask some of the ketchupy taste. You may add a bit of sugar to cut the lemon's acidity.

Salt

Add a peeled, thinly sliced potato to the salty dish and boil until the potato is transparent. Remove the potato slices.

or

If fish is too salty, add vinegar to the cooking liquid.

or

For a tomato dish, add more peeled tomatoes to absorb the salt. Leave in dish if appropriate.

or

For items like soup, stew, or tomato sauce, add pinches of brown sugar to taste.

Tomato

Add lemon juice to mask some of the tomato taste. Add a bit of sugar to cut the lemon's acidity.

Too Spicy

In the pot, add salt.

On the tongue, lips, or mouth, a little sugar, buttermilk, milk, bread, or crackers will help neutralize the spiciness.

Measurement Equivalents

Here is a list of commonly used measuring equivalents for the kitchen, including:

Baking Pans

Food Measuring Equivalents

Metric Equivalents

Temperatures

Baking Pan Sizes

Note: Adjust baking times when changing pan sizes.

Cake Pans, Rectangular

8" x 8" x 2"
- = 6 cups
- = 20 cm x 20 cm x 5 cm

9" x 9" x 1½"
- = 6 cups
- = 23 cm x 23 cm x 4 cm

9" x 9" x 2"
- = 7 cups
- = 23 cm x 23 cm x 5 cm

Cake Pans, Rectangular, *continued*

13" x 9" x 2"

- = 10 cups
- = 33 cm x 23 cm x 5 cm

Cake Pans, Round

8" x $1\frac{1}{2}$"

- = 4 cups
- = 20 cm x 4 cm

9" x $1\frac{1}{2}$"

- = 6 cups
- = 23 cm x 4 cm

Loaf Pans

$8\frac{1}{2}$" x $4\frac{1}{2}$" x $2\frac{1}{2}$"

- = 6 cups
- = 22 cm x 11 cm x 6 cm

9" x 5" x 3"

- = 8 cups
- = 23 cm x 13 cm x 8 cm

Pie Pans

8" x $1\frac{1}{4}$"

- = 3 cups, level
- = $4\frac{1}{2}$ cups, mounded
- = 20 cm x 3 cm

Pie Pans, *continued*

9" x 1½"
- = 4 cups, level
- = 5 to 6 cups, mounded
- = 23 cm x 4 cm

Springform Pans

8" x 3"
- = 10 cups
- = 20 cm x 8 cm

9" x 3"
- = 11 cups
- = 23 cm x 9 cm

10" x 3¾ "
- = 12 cups
- = 25 cm x 10 cm

Tube Pans or Ring Molds

8½" x 2¼"
- = 4½ cups
- = 22 cm x 6 cm

7½" x 3"
- = 6 cups
- = 19 cm x 8 cm

9¼" x 2¾"
- = 8 cups
- = 23 cm x 7 cm

Food Measuring Equivalents

Dry Measures

1 pinch = $\frac{1}{8}$ teaspoon, approximately

$\frac{1}{2}$ tablespoon = $1\frac{1}{2}$ teaspoons

3 teaspoons = 1 tablespoon

$\frac{1}{4}$ cup = 4 tablespoons

$\frac{1}{3}$ cup = 5 tablespoons + 1 teaspoon

$\frac{3}{8}$ cup = 6 tablespoons

$\frac{1}{2}$ cup = 8 tablespoons

$\frac{2}{3}$ cup = 10 tablespoons + 2 teaspoons

$\frac{3}{4}$ cup = 12 tablespoons

1 cup = 16 tablespoons

4 cups = 1 quart

8 quarts = 1 peck*

4 pecks = 1 bushel*

* for large fruits and vegetables, not berries

Liquid Measures

1 dash = a few drops, approximately

1 tablespoon = 3 teaspoons

1 tablespoon = ½ fluid ounce

1 fluid ounce = 2 tablespoons

1 jigger = 3 tablespoons or 1½ fluid ounces

¼ cup = 4 tablespoons or 2 fluid ounces

½ cup = 8 tablespoons or 4 fluid ounces

1 cup = 16 tablespoons or 8 fluid ounces

1 pint = 2 cups or 16 fluid ounces

1 quart = 2 pints or 32 fluid ounces

1 gallon = 4 quarts or 64 fluid ounces

Fluid Ounces	=	Milliliters
1		30
2		60
4		120
6		180
8 (1 cup)		235
16 (1 pint)		475
32 (1 quart)		945

Note: 1 quart = .946 liter

1 liter = 1.057 quarts

Metric Equivalents

Ounces	=	Grams
1		28
2		57
3		85
4		113
5		142
6		170
7		198
8		227
9		255
10		284
11		312
12		340
13		368
14		397
15		425
16		454

Grams	=	Ounces
1		.035
50		1.75
100		3.5
250		8.75
500		17.5
750		26.25
1000 (1 kilogram)		35 (2.21 lbs.)

Metric Equivalents

Pounds	=	Kilograms
1		.45
2		.91
3		1.4
4		1.8
5		2.3
6		2.7
7		3.2
8		3.5
9		4.1
10		4.5

Kilograms	=	Pounds
1		2.2
2		4.4
3		6.6
4		8.8
5		11

Temperature Equivalents

	Degrees Fahrenheit	=	Degrees Celsius (Centigrade)
Room Temperature	70		21
Lukewarm	90		32
Water's Boiling Point	212		100
Low or Cool Oven	250		120
Slow Oven	300		150
Moderately Slow Oven	325		165
Moderate Oven	350		180
Moderately Hot Oven	375		190
Hot Oven	400		205
Very Hot Oven	450–500		230–260
Broil	550		290

Household Formulas

You probably know what it feels like to be standing in the supermarket, not wanting to spend a small fortune on the lastest specialty cleanser just to see if maybe it works.

Remember how your grandmother used to give you helpful cleaning hints? Only now you can't recall any of them.

Look down this list, and chances are you'll find a tried-and-true recipe for just what you need. Many of these substitutions for cleansers are non-toxic alternatives—and thus kinder to both people and the environment.

Air Freshener

Pour vinegar into an uncovered dish.

All-Purpose Cleanser

½ cup Borax

1 gallon warm water

or

½ cup ammonia

¼ cup vinegar

2 tablespoons baking soda

1 gallon warm water

Note: Good for floors.

All-Purpose Cleanser, *continued*

or

½ cup ammonia

½ cup washing soda

1 gallon warm water

Bathroom Cleanser

Dip damp sponge in baking soda.

Black Lacquer Cleanser

Dip a cloth in a strong tea solution and rub well.

Brass Cleanser

Rub hard with lemon juice and salt. Or spread with ketchup, let stand 10 minutes, and then rub hard.

Breadbox Cleanser

2 tablespoons vinegar in 1 quart water. *Note:* Deters mold, too.

Carpet Deodorizer

1 cup baking soda or 1 cup cornstarch

Sprinkle on carpet. Wait 30 minutes and vacuum.

Copper Cleanser

Spread with a paste of lemon juice, salt, and flour, or spread with ketchup. Let stand 10 minutes and rub hard.

Crystal Cleanser

Use a mixture of half rubbing alcohol, half water. Do not rinse.

Disinfectant

Use $\frac{1}{2}$ cup Borax in 1 gallon hot water.

Drain Freshener

Pour $\frac{1}{2}$ cup baking soda down the drain. After 2 minutes pour in $\frac{1}{2}$ cup vinegar followed by 2 quarts of boiling water.

Drain Opener

Dump 1 cup baking soda down drain, followed by 1 cup vinegar. Cover drain. When fizzing stops, pour boiling water down drain.

Electric Iron Stain Remover

Use equal parts vinegar and salt.

Floor Cleaner

$\frac{1}{2}$ cup vinegar
$\frac{1}{2}$ gallon warm water

Floor Shiner

$\frac{1}{2}$ cup cornstarch
1 gallon lukewarm water

Furniture Polish

$\frac{1}{3}$ cup boiled linseed oil
$\frac{1}{3}$ cup turpentine
$\frac{1}{3}$ cup vinegar

or

$\frac{2}{3}$ cup olive or vegetable oil
$\frac{1}{3}$ cup lemon juice

Hard Water Deposit Remover

Soak item in white vinegar or a half-and-half solution of white vinegar and water.

Mildew Remover

$\frac{1}{2}$ cup vinegar

$\frac{1}{2}$ cup Borax

Warm water

Non-Stick Pan Cleanser

Use baking soda on a non-abrasive scouring pad.

Oven Cleaner, for non-self-cleaning ovens

Pour $\frac{1}{2}$ cup ammonia into a bowl. Set in cold oven overnight. Next morning, mix the ammonia with 1 quart warm water and wipe off inside of oven.

or

Mix equal parts baking soda and salt. Scrub with a damp sponge.

Pot and Pan Cleanser

Soak in white vinegar for 30 minutes.

Refrigerator Cleanser

1 tablespoon Borax

1 quart water

or

1 teaspoon baking soda

1 quart water

Scouring Powder

Use baking soda.

Silver Cleanser

Make paste of baking soda and water. Apply with damp sponge or cloth and continue rubbing until clean.

or

Use toothpaste and a soft-bristled toothbrush.

Spot and Blood Remover

$1/2$ cup Borax

2 cups cold water

Stainless Steel Cleanser

Use ammonia and hot water, mixed with a mild, non-chlorinated cleanser.

or

To remove spots, rub with a cloth dampened with white vinegar.

Toilet Bowl Cleanser

4 tablespoons baking soda

1 cup vinegar

Tub and Tile Cleanser

Rub with half a lemon dipped in Borax.

Window Cleanser

Mix $1/2$ cup white or cider vinegar in $1/2$ gallon water. Spray on windows and wipe with crumpled newspaper.

Window Cleanser, *continued*

or

Use ½ cup cornstarch in 2 quarts warm water.

or

Use 1 tablespoon ammonia in 2 cups water. Wear protective gloves while you clean.

Woodwork Cleanser

1 teaspoon white vinegar

1 quart water

Woodwork (Varnished), Furniture, or Glass Cleanser

Tea, steeped 30 to 40 minutes

About the Authors

BECKY SUE EPSTEIN is a food and wine writer based in Los Angeles, where she serves on the board of the American Institute of Wine and Food. She is the author of *The Dessert Course,* scheduled for publication in 1992.

HILARY DOLE KLEIN is a columnist for the *The Santa Barbara Independent,* a restaurant reviewer for *The Los Angeles Times,* and the Santa Barbara restaurant correspondent for KABC Radio in Los Angeles. She has written and edited seven books, including *Santa Barbara Cooks* and *Tiny Game Hunting.*